Ten Steps to a One-Place Study

Janet Few

Published by Blue Poppy Publishing 2020

ISBN 978-1-911438-18-2

Ten Steps to a One-Place Study

Janet Few

Blue Poppy Publishing

I would like to thank Martha Barnard and Janet Barrie for their comments on the first draft of this booklet. Any errors that remain are my own.

Contents

What is a One-Place Study?

One-place studies are a fascinating blend of family history and local history. This form of micro-research is becoming increasingly popular amongst genealogists and local historians. A one-place study involves investigating a small geographical area in minute detail, researching the inhabitants, the buildings and the institutions within that place, as well as the events that took place there. These studies are often undertaken by family historians who are seeking context for their ancestors; ancestors who may have lived in the same area for several generations. Alternatively, local historians might focus their research on the inhabitants of the community that they are interested in; that too becomes a one-place study.

One-place studies do not just involve collecting data. They entail using that data to learn about the inhabitants, both collectively and individually. Once you have amassed a body of information you will be able to draw conclusions about what was happening in that community at a particular point in time. One-place studies are an intensely personal brand of history and as such, are a wonderful way of encouraging others to engage with their history and heritage.

Although careful, accurate research is the backbone of a one-place study, there are no hard and fast rules. This booklet outlines ten steps, that will lead you to a successful one-place study. Some steps you will climb once, perhaps quite swiftly, others will be ongoing. Although the precise sources that are available will vary, it is intended that these techniques can be followed regardless of where in the world your place is located. For this reason, what follows refers to types of record, rather than specific sources. You will need to turn to other local and family history guides for more information about exactly what is available for your area and how that might be accessed.

Step 1 - Making Choices

Choosing your boundaries

In order to carry out a one-place study you must first choose a place. If you have read this far, you probably already have a place in mind. You may even have made a start on your study. If you are still deciding which place to investigate, or if you are wondering whether you have made the right choice, here are some things to consider.

1. Where will my place be?

Places can be anywhere that you choose. Ideally, they will have a clearly defined boundary. In a British context, a parish is the most common unit for a study. There are other options. For example, you might want to choose a street, a single dwelling, a cemetery, a school or a factory. The size of your chosen place will make a difference to the way in which you carry out your research. It may be practical to aim to discover and name everyone associated with a community that has a population of a few hundred at any one time but this is unlikely to be feasible with a larger town. It is sensible to have some idea of the size of the population that you will be working with before making your final decision.

It does help if the boundaries that you choose are reflected in the records that you will be using. It may be easy to identify a street in a directory or a census return but it will probably be more difficult to associate church register entries with a specific road, rather than the wider community. This is not a reason not to choose a street, just something to be aware of.

2. Is someone already studying this place?

Most people prefer to choose an 'unadopted' place, one that is not already being investigated in great detail. Others though, might prefer to work collaboratively and build on existing research that is being undertaken by an individual or group. There are a number of ways of finding out about existing work. Perhaps the simplest is to put 'history of *place name*' into a search engine. You are looking for publications, websites and societies that might indicate that someone is already studying the place that you have in mind.

There are two main websites that will tell you if a one-place study is already underway for a particular community.
Society for One-Place Studies http://one-place-studies.org/studies
One-Place Studies Directory www.oneplacestudy.org
You could also go to Cyndi's List www.cyndislist.com and then drill down to your area of interest.

There are a number of specific websites to check, depending on the country where your prospective place lies.

In the United Kingdom
Local History Online www.local-history.co.uk/index.html - a list of many but not all, local history groups.

The British Association for Local History www.balh.co.uk
The Community Archives and Heritage Group www.communityarchives.org.uk
Blatchford, Robert and Elizabeth Blatchford Family and Local History Handbook (Robert Blatchford Publishing Ltd. issued periodically), see www.genealogical.co.uk. They also produce an Irish version.
In addition, keep an eye out for online parish clerks (OPCs). These are individuals with a particular interest in a parish. The scheme is more popular in the south-west of England but is spreading. Links to OPCs are usually found on the GENUKI page for the appropriate parish www.genuki.org.uk. For more information and links see www.ukbmd.org.uk/online_parish_clerk

In Canada
Our Roots/Nos Racines www.ourroots.ca

In the United States
Preservation Directory www.preservationdirectory.com/HistoricalPreservation/Home.aspx
American Association for State and Local History https://aaslh.org

In Australia
Australian family history and historical societies https://guides.slv.vic.gov.au/c.php?g=245303&p=1633146
Internet History Resources www.ihr.com.au/societies.html

In New Zealand
New Zealand Federation of Historical Societies Inc.
www.nzhistoricalsocieties.org.nz

It is also a good idea to enquire at libraries and archives that are local to your prospective place, to see if they are aware of any work being done.

3. How much data is available and how will I access this?

Record survival is not uniform. There will be a wealth of data for some places and very little for others. It is a good idea to have a quick check for what survives for the main classes of record (such as church records, censuses, gravestones, newspapers and wills) before you begin.

You also need to consider how you will access these records. Many people do conduct one-place studies from a distance, even from another country. This is only practical if there is a reasonable amount online for your place, if you can arrange periodic visits, or if you can cultivate a local assistant to visit the archives on your behalf.

4. Am I going to work alone?

Having just mentioned the possibility of an assistant, it is a good idea to decide if you plan to be a solo studier, or if you would welcome sharing the load. This is really a matter of both practicality and personal preference. Some one-place studiers begin on their own and later gather a group around them, perhaps going as far as forming a club or society.

5. What place am I most interested in?

Although this is the last question, it is the most important one. Your one-place study will be a huge investment of time, energy and probably money. It needs to be a place that you can love and sustain a long-term interest in. Most studiers choose their home community, or a place that has significant ancestral connections.

Choosing your timeframe

Many one-place studiers restrict the timeframe for their research. There may be several reasons for this. Perhaps the community was not inhabited before a certain date, records may not survive, or the studier has decided not to include recent material due to data protection concerns. Others limit the timescale in order to make the study more manageable and this can be a very good idea, especially at first. You can always extend your date-span later.

Choosing your starting point

Tackling a new project can be daunting but remember, you do not have to do it all at once. In order not to be overwhelmed, you need to decide where you will begin. There are three likely starting points for a one-place study.

1. Beginning with a source

This is the traditional starting point and probably the easiest option. So, you might choose to photograph and transcribe the memorials in the graveyard, index the church registers, or look at a street directory. For countries that have surviving censuses, it is common to begin by indexing a single census return. In this way, you very quickly amass details about both individuals and dwellings and begin to link one with another (step five). It is also easy to expand on this by moving on to look at the censuses before and after your initial return. The only drawback of a source as a starting point is that the results have little wider appeal. You will have created a database; a valuable database it is true but one of the other starting points might result in a more interesting initial product.

2. Beginning with a timespan

You might decide to begin by looking at a narrow date span, perhaps no more than a decade. You can then use a variety of sources to build up a picture of your place at that time. This is more involved than option one as you will perhaps still be indexing that census return but you will also look at newspaper reports, church records and gravestones for the same period. There will be other sources that may also apply and you can gradually incorporate more but the crucial aspect of this technique is to combine sources to give a more rounded impression of the place. If you do this you will have very swiftly moved to step seven, albeit in a limited way. This starting point creates possibilities very early on in your study. You will soon be equipped to talk, write, present or exhibit about such topics as '*place name* in the 1880s'.

The disadvantage of this method is that you will need to revisit many of these sources in order to look, for example, at the gravestones, or the baptism register for a wider date-span when you extend your research beyond this initial time period. You will also need to keep meticulous records, so that you know what has already been searched. This is important whatever approach you choose but particularly so with this one.

3. **Beginning with a theme**

This involves picking a topic, such as '*place name* at war', or 'education in *place name*' and looking at all relevant sources. This is probably something that you would normally leave until you have worked your way to step seven, treading on all the intervening steps in between. Sometimes though, community events prompt you to start your study in this way. For example, a number of projects that centred round the centenary of world war one, went on to become wider one-place studies.

Step 2 - Reconstructing your Place

This step is all about gaining an impression of what your place would have looked like at different points in time.

You need to think about:
Geographical features: terrain, rivers, lakes, flora and fauna
Man-made features: buildings, roads, street furniture

This can be achieved in several ways.

Field Walking

The best way to create a mental image of your place is to walk the roads and fields yourself. This is not always practical, particularly if you do not live close by. The next best thing is to make a virtual visit using Google street view. If you are visiting in person, take photographs, so that you have a record of how your place looks today. If you are unable to do this yourself, see if you can find someone local to do this on your behalf. Geograph www.geograph.org is a good source of images available under Creative Commons Licence and is expanding to cover several countries. Study the built landscape to see if you can judge roughly how old structures might be. Look for alterations, such as signs of former industrial buildings having been repurposed as dwellings, or two houses that have been knocked into one.

Maps

Obtaining a series of maps is essential to picturing your place. Ideally, you want large scale maps that will show individual buildings and other features, as well as maps of the wider area, which will enable you to understand how your community related to its surroundings. Maps that were produced at different dates are invaluable when you are trying to understand how your place has changed over time.

There are many sources of old maps online. Although this booklet is designed to be appropriate for worldwide studies, the following National Library of Scotland site http://maps.nls.uk/index.html is worth highlighting. This allows access to maps that go beyond Scotland. Wherever your place is, you may find that there are retailers selling facsimiles of old maps.

You may also decide to produce sketch maps of your own, that can be annotated with dates of construction, or inhabitants' names.

Books and Websites

Seek out local history books and websites that cover your place, or a larger area that includes your place. Three series that are very important in a British context are:

The Victoria County Histories
https://www.history.ac.uk/research/victoria-county-history

The General View of Agriculture Surveys, which were produced between the 1790s and 1810s https://en.wikipedia.org/wiki/General_View_of_Agriculture_county_surveys

The Scottish Statistical Accounts, which are accessible and downloadable online https://stataccscot.edina.ac.uk (click on the map).

Do not neglect the many local histories and books of historical photographs that may have been privately published with short print-runs. Be aware however that this kind of publication can vary in quality.

Websites, Facebook Groups and Pinterest Boards for The History of *place name* are increasingly common and tend to be most useful for more recent history.

Images

Seek out photographs, paintings and engravings of your place. Try to identify the descendants of former inhabitants, using the same methods as family historians employ when they are tracing distant living relatives. By contacting them, you may acquire copies of photographs for individuals who used to live in your place.

It may be that there are moving images of your place. Make enquires at regional film archives.

Step 3 - Populating your Place

Now it is time to add some people to the picture that you have created for your place. An understanding of overall population trends can be very useful when you are trying to work out what is going on in particular community. It is also important to populate your place at an individual level.

At a Community Level

See if you can access population statistics for your place at different points in time.

Here are some websites that might help.

United States www.census.gov
Canada www.statcan.gc.ca
Australia www.abs.gov.au
New Zealand www.stats.govt.nz
United Kingdom www.histpop.org
United Kingdom www.visionofbritain.org.uk
Ireland C20th www.cso.ie/en/index.html
Scotland www.nrscotland.gov.uk

If the information is available, creating population profiles for different dates is also useful. This means dividing the population by age and gender. This becomes more meaningful if you can investigate any changes over time. Demographers often produce graphs known as 'population profiles'. You can do this on paper but there are several versions of instructions for producing population pyramids on a computer:

https://excelchamps.com/blog/pyramid-chart
www.excel-exercise.com/population-pyramid
https://iase-web.org/islp/apps/gov_stats_graphing/PopulationPyramids/PopulationPyramids-Instructions.pdf

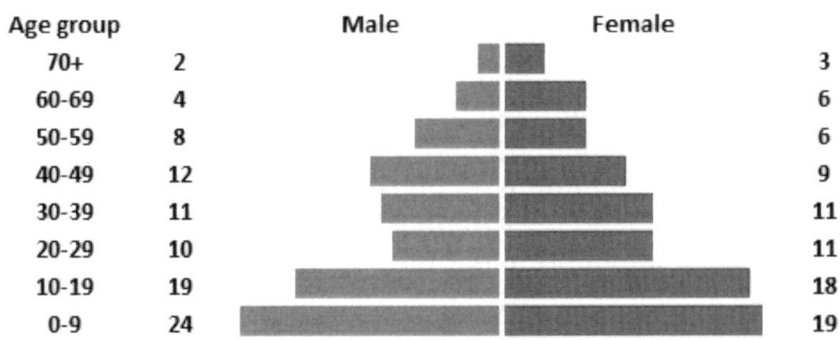

The, probably non-existent, 'average' population pyramid is a symmetrical triangular shape. If the pyramid for your place deviates from this, there are implications. A pyramid that goes in in the middle (those aged in their 20s – 40s), is losing the economically active section of the population, so is likely to be in decline. If your pyramid bulges at this point, it is what is known as a 'receiving community', drawing workers in from elsewhere and is likely to have a thriving economy.

At an Individual Level

All but the very largest one-place studies involve creating some kind of database or card index of the individuals associated with the community. There are probably as many versions of these as there are one-place studiers. Ideally, you need to make a decision early on about what you will include, as it is much easier than trying to add additional fields at a later date. Some studiers will include only basic details, others will have many fields. Just remember that multiple fields can be unwieldy and involve much swiping from side to side as you try to use your computer-generated database.

Here are some of the fields that you might consider:

Reference number
Surname
Forename(s)
Date of birth
Birthplace
Father's name
Mother's name
Baptism date
Place of baptism
Date of marriage (you might wish to allow for more than one marriage)
Place of marriage
Spouse(s)
Occupation

Residence (you may decide to allow multiple fields for this – some one-place studiers will have fields for each available census for example).
Date of death
Place of death
Date of burial
Place of burial

You are likely to want to record the sources of this information as well. As you can see, this will rapidly become a very wide database. There is no easy solution to this and every studier will need to decide how they might manage all the data they collect about the inhabitants of their place.

It is also interesting to see if you can find details of how many dwellings, or households, there were at different dates. If census returns survive, these are a useful way of acquiring this data. You may decide that you want to create a dwellings database, recording when homes were built and demolished and who was living there at various points in time.

Step 4 - Collecting Data from Specific Sources

Acknowledging that one-place studies are worldwide, this step does not provide details of country specific records. Instead, it draws your attention to the categories of record that you may be able to use. Consult 'how to' family and local history research guides, or other learning materials, for the country or region where your place lies. These will give you the information that you need about the particular records that might be available and how to access them.

Newspapers

Step two involved gathering information about the physical space. Step four will see you collecting data about the people, the dwellings, other buildings, institutions and events. Most of the sources that you interrogate will provide information about more than one of these categories. Newspapers are a case in point, as there you will find information about all of these aspects. Even very small communities will appear in the local press. If you search the index of an online newspaper archive, unless you have a very tiny place, you are likely to come up with a large number of references, probably more than you can process in several lifetimes. Here are just some ways of accessing newspapers online:

Britain - www.britishnewspaperarchive.co.uk
Australia - https://trove.nla.gov.au/newspaper
Unites States - http://chroniclingamerica.loc.gov

Canada –
https://sites.google.com/site/onlinenewspapersite/Home/can
http://libguides.bgsu.edu/CanadianNewspapers
www.ourontario.ca/demo/news.html
New Zealand - http://paperspast.natlib.govt.nz

Although searches may be very slow, do not neglect newspapers that have not yet been digitised. Rather than attempting to do blanket searches, it is likely that you will use these for targeted research regarding a particular person or event.

Personal Records

Personal records are probably the most difficult to acquire because they are frequently in private hands. These take several forms.

1. Oral Testimony

If you are able to interview long-term residents of your place to record their memories, that is ideal. You may also wish to track down and speak to those who no longer live in the community but who have memories to share. Conducting an oral history project is not always straightforward. These accounts are the copyright of your interviewee and you are advised to get a written agreement, outlining how the interview will be used and granting permission for you to do this. This avoids problems if relatives are less than comfortable with how you have used granny's memories. It is also important to be sensitive about details of people, who might be mentioned in these discussions, who may still be alive.

Oral history has been popular for half a century, so do investigate if interviews have been carried out in preceding decades. Sound archives may hold material that could be useful.

2. Diaries, Letters and Memoirs

These provide a unique insight into the life of your place but can be very difficult to locate and access. By advertising the existence of your study as widely as possible (step nine), you maximise your chances of being given the opportunity to view these gems.

3. Artefacts

Some one-place studiers collect three-dimensional artefacts related to their place. These can take many forms and might include commemorative china, promotional or advertising items produced by local businesses, archaeological finds, samplers, postcards addressed to inhabitants of their place, bill heads, school prizes and a whole host of other items. The online auction site eBay allows you to save a search term and receive a notification when something relating to your place is offered for sale. You may want to acquire as many of these objects as possible, or you may be content with establishing a virtual museum by photographing them instead. You might also seek out such objects that are in private hands and ask if you can photograph them. Don't forget to visit established local museums to see if they have any relevant artefacts.

Vital Records

There are several types of record that fall into this category. Vital records encompass anything where the primary purpose was to record a birth, marriage or death. In most countries, the recording of these events by the civil authorities (civil registration) was preceded by the religious authorities recording baptisms, marriages and burials.

You will need to seek out the registers for all the religious groups who had places of worship in your place. These may be in local or national archives, still with the congregations, or, sadly, lost. The good news is that this type of record has been prioritised by the online data providers, so there is online access to many church records. Do not forget that there may be smaller congregations whose records are not available in this way. Some places of worship may have amalgamated, so be aware that the records of a closed building could be held with those of the new congregations.

Gravestones are another way in which death or burial can be recorded. At some point, you will probably want to record the memorials in your place, if it contains a burial ground. If it does not, you will have the problem of distinguishing the inhabitants of your place from others who came from the broader community that is served by a cemetery or burial ground. As grave markers deteriorate over time, recording gravestones may be something that you decide to do sooner rather than later.

Indexes of registered births, marriages and deaths are available online for many countries, provinces or regions. Unfortunately, the geographical units that these are arranged by are normally much larger than a studied place. It is usually very difficult, or impossible, to work out which events within the wider area relate to inhabitants of your place. All you can do, is identify an inhabitant from other sources and then seek out their birth, marriage and death on an individual basis. Actual birth, marriage and death certificates are rarely freely available and purchasing them for all the residents of your place will be budget breaking. You might however be able to trace descendants of the inhabitants of your place. With luck, they may have certificates for their ancestors and will be willing to share the information.

Records of Residence

1. Censuses

Censuses are a key tool for a one-place studier. Most researchers will use one or more census returns early on in their study. Not only are they a good way of associating people with a specific place (step five) but they give additional information that allows you to study topics such as occupations or migration on an individual and community level. Using censuses, you are able to investigate family groups and this will be key in researching the pedigrees of your more recent inhabitants.

2. Directories

Directories perform a similar function to censuses but are less informative. They do however enable you to link named individuals with particular addresses. Trade directories will also provide details about occupations but you rarely find information about anyone apart from the head of household from them. One advantage of directories is that they were produced more frequently than censuses, in some instances annually, so you get a fuller picture of changes of occupier. Be aware that there was a time lag between data collection and the publication of a directory. So, a directory dated 1871 may be a more accurate reflection of the situation in 1870, or even 1869.

Records of Education and Occupation

Like most of the classes of record discussed in this step, what is available in different countries varies. As regards records of education, depending where your place is, you might find school year books, admissions' registers, log-books or school magazines that you can consult. There are also likely to be references to school events in newspapers.

For an overview of the occupational profile in your place, trade directories and census returns are the most helpful sources. Using these, you can build up a detailed picture of the types of employment that prevailed in your place at a particular point in time. Do look at different time frames, to see if the occupational structure changes within your community. It is also interesting to consider how topography, geology, climate and transport links affect the occupations that predominate in your place. Sources relating to occupations might include company archives for a specific employer in your place, trade union records, apprenticeship records or even lists of the brands used by sheep farmers to identify their flock.

Records of Taxation

Taxation is and has been, a fact of life in all communities, worldwide. Taxes are usually administered at a national level and the records are therefore likely to be in national archives, if they are not online. In some countries, taxation records go back for many centuries. The returns are usually arranged geographically, making them suitable for one-place studies. Often, these records will be little more than a list of names and amounts paid but even this enables a named person to be associated with your place at a specific date. If the tax levied varies between individuals, it will also provide an idea of relative wealth.

Inventive governments have taxed many things. Of use for the purposes of a one-place study are the head or 'poll' taxes, which were usually applied only to adult men or householders. The other common tax is one on land. These are far from being the limits of taxation. In Britain for example, at different times, hearths, servants, windows, dogs and hair-powder have all been taxed; unfortunately, not all the records survive. National governments may also have undertaken valuations for specific purposes, for example, in times of war.

There are also rates that will have been levied at a local level. These might include contributions towards the maintenance of the highways, 'sanitary' rates, for providing water and sewage disposal, or more general local taxes. Surviving records are likely to be at town or regional archives, or local studies libraries, or still held by the local authorities themselves.

Records of Landownership

Records of landownership vary greatly from country to country. Some of the tax records mentioned above will distinguish between owners and occupiers. If your place was settled within the last few hundred years, there may be records of grants of land. Individual leases are invaluable but as they were often held in private hands, survival is patchy and not all will have made their way into record repositories. More recently, there may be records relating to planning permission.

Records of Local Government

Historic electoral rolls or voters' lists may be available for your place. These will usually associate named individuals with a specific address. Other council or local authority records, such as minutes of meetings, might also be useful. It is from these that you may learn of decisions that would have affected your place, such as resolutions to install street lighting or a water supply.

Records of the Fortunate and the Less Fortunate

Probate records may be available for the richer inhabitants of your place. Some wills will be indexed by name only, rather than place. In this instance you will have to consider each death that occurred in your place and search for wills on an individual basis. This is well worth doing as, apart from family information, there may be behests to local charities and mentions of servants and other non-relatives.

The less fortunate people in your place may have left records of their own. Perhaps there will be details of their support by church or state. Seek out workhouse and asylum records.

Court records will provide information about residents from all walks of life. Like many other records, these may be difficult to search by place. It is likely that the first clue that the inhabitants of your place were involved in a court case, either as accuser, accused, arresting officer, victim or witness, will be through an account in the newspapers. If you can track down these records, they will make an interesting addition to your one-place study.

Records of the Movement of People

The character of your place is dictated by those who move in and those who leave. As mentioned above, censuses that give details of birthplaces, provide you with information about the origins of those who arrive in your community. Depending on the country in which your place lies, it may also be possible to search censuses by birthplace, to find the destinations of individuals who have left your place to reside elsewhere.

Passenger lists and records of immigration centres might also help you to track down the migration histories of those who spent time living in your place.

Step 5 - Making Connections

One of the most exciting parts of a one-place study is making connections. These connections are likely to take several forms.

Between People

Those who have come to one-place studies having been genealogists will be used to making connections between people. In a small country community and to a lesser extent, in an urban setting, many of the inhabitants will be related to each other. Making connections between people is about investigating the family relationships that link the inhabitants of your place. This is achieved by creating family trees, in the same way as you would for your own personal family history. Most genealogical software packages will allow you to enter unrelated families in the same file. This way, if you do find a connection, they can be joined together at a later date.

It may be that the common ancestor of two of your inhabitants is an individual who has no connection with your place. You will have to make your own decision about how wide you cast the net, looking for links. For example, you may decide to take the pedigree back one or two generations outside the community in search of a relationship.

Between People and Places

Intrinsic to one-place studies is the concept of putting people in their geographical context. You will already have identified individuals who are associated with your place as a whole but now it is time to link people with specific buildings. One of the reasons why censuses, or in their absence, directories, make good starting points for one-place studies is that you are immediately associating named people with their homes.

Most one-place studiers compile databases. As mentioned above, creating a database of all those associated with the community is common, as is documenting the residential history of each home. If your place is large, this will not be practical but you may decide to do this for a selection of the properties in your place.

Of course, people are not just linked to the buildings in which they lived. For example, you might decide to find out who was associated with a church, a school, a factory, a war memorial or a graveyard.

People and Events

One-place studies are also about the events that took place within that community. Newspaper reports may help you to discover who was present on certain occasions. You might find accounts of prize winners at the agricultural show, performers at the school concert, or speakers at a political meeting. Each time you can associate a named individual with a specific event you are learning a little more about their life.

Step 6 - Analysing your Data

Analysing your data involves taking a single source and using the information that it contains to explore a particular topic. Here are just a few examples.

1. Use a trade directory to investigate occupational structure in your place at a particular point in time. You can look at the numbers engaged in specific occupations, or group occupations together to compare numbers involved in agriculture, retail, heavy industry, service industries and so on.

2. Use a church burial register to look at ages at death and changes over time.

3. Use a census return to examine household structure. How many people were there in a single dwelling? Who made up the household? Were they nuclear families or extended families?

4. Use a tax return to consider the relative wealth of the inhabitants of your place.

5. Use the places of birth in a census return to begin to study migration patterns.

6. Use sources such as land grants or a tithe schedule to investigate land ownership.

Almost all of these mini projects can be built upon to extend your understanding of a theme, as described in step seven.

Step 7 - Synthesise your Data

Step seven is an extension of step six. It involves drawing on multiple sources to examine a theme or a short time period. This is about much more than collecting data and is likely to result in some kind of narrative report or article about your findings. Alternatively, or additionally, it may culminate in a community event or celebration, or an exhibition.

This type of research might be prompted by a specific research question about your place, or a hypothesis about a trend that you have observed. This list of possible questions is endless but in this way, you might set out to understand such things as why the population in your place fell dramatically at a particular time, or how improved transport links impacted on migration.

Here are just some of the themes that you might choose to investigate, with very brief details of what that might entail.

1. Faith in my place

Identify and examine the history of all the places of worship in your place. Research the biographies of the key individuals associated with these places of worship, such as founders and leaders.

2. Education in my place

Investigate all the options for formal education in your place. Research the histories of schools and colleges. Research the biographies of the key individuals associated with these educational establishments, such as founders and educators.

3. Population Change in my place

Collate information about demographic trends. Consider if these follow the regional or national pattern. Look for reasons for population rises and declines, or irregularities in the balance between the genders or age groups.

4. My place at War

Investigate the impact of a specific war or wars on your place. Research the stories of those inhabitants who served. Study any campaigns, battles or war damage that occurred in your place.

5. Fertility and Infant Mortality in my place

Use vital records, census returns and other sources to investigate family size and infant mortality rates in your place.

6. My place in a Specific Decade

Choose a particular decade and use all available sources to build up a picture of life in your place during those ten years.

7. Migration and my place

Investigate the geographical origins of those who moved into your place and the destinations of those who left. You might also look at the occupations, ages, faith and migration companions of those who moved in and out, to see if you can identify any trends.

8. Occupations in my place

Look at the occupation profile of your place and how this alters over time. Try to identify possible reasons for any changes. Research the history of key employers or businesses in your place. See what you can find out about the processes involved in the main industries that are represented in the community. Consider how self-sufficient the community would have been at different points in time.

9. Leisure, Services and Institutions in my place

This could be three separate projects but there is some overlap, so you might decide to combine them. In all three instances, consider change over time.

Identify the leisure opportunities in your place for the inhabitants at different points in time. Newspapers and directories will be key to this work but also consider personal reminiscences and maps as potential sources of information. You are looking for evidence of clubs and societies as well as opportunities for social gatherings, such as theatres, dance halls or sports facilities.

Research the services that were available in your place by identifying such things as transport links, hospitals, libraries, parks, schools, places of worship, shops and markets.

Concentrate on the institutions in your place. Research the history of any buildings that were not residential, such as mills, mines, factories, places of worship, shops, civic buildings, schools and railway stations. Compare the availability of such institutions at different points in time.

Step 8 - Contextualising your Findings

Whilst all the information you are gathering, analysing and synthesising about your place is intrinsically interesting, you can go further than just viewing your place in isolation. The findings for your place need to be set in the context of what is going on elsewhere in the region, the country or even the world. You need to be asking yourself how typical your place was. Was the experience of living there similar to that in places elsewhere, or was it distinctive in some way? What might be the reasons for any differences?

See if you can collaborate with other one-place studiers to compare your findings. It is a good idea to look at another community that you would expect to be similar and one that might be very different. So, if you are studying a rural community in the south of the country, can you compare it to a similar one in the north? When you are looking for a community that is different in nature to your own, it is often a good idea to choose one that is reasonably close geographically. In a British context, this might mean one in the same county. If your community is in a mining area, how different was life in a nearby fishing community? Of course, you could always just start another one-place study yourself and be your own collaborator!

The Society for One-place Studies www.one-place-studies.org coordinates regular, themed 'shared endeavours', which are an ideal opportunity for comparing and collaborating. The Family and Community Historical

Research Society www.fachrs.com also encourages this way of working but their projects are limited to British research. You do not have to be part of an official collaborative project. You could approach another one-place studier on a one-to-one basis. One-place studies are carried out in very different ways so, if possible, find someone whose methods are compatible with your own, or a researcher who is working on a similar theme.

Step 9 – Spreading the Word

It is improbable that you will want to keep your one-place study to yourself. The more widely you spread the word, the more likely you are to make contact with those who can make a contribution. There will be people who have photographs of your place, memories to share, or diaries kept by former inhabitants. By publicising your study, you stand a better chance of finding them. There are a number of things you can do.

Publicising your Study

1. **Get your study listed online**

The One-Place Studies Directory www.oneplacestudy.org offer free listings.

The Society for One-Place Studies www.one-place-studies.org requires the payment of a small annual subscription but this will allow you to put not just a short profile of your study on their website but also an in-depth account, such as this www.one-place-studies.org/resources/in-depth-reports/in-depth-bucks-mills.
Membership of the society also brings other benefits www.one-place-studies.org/about/why-join-the-society-for-one-place-studies.

If you have a web presence, then submit a link for inclusion on Cyndi's List www.cyndislist.com.

If you have a study in the United Kingdom, ask if it can be listed on the appropriate parish page at www.genuki.org.uk.

2. Inform institutions in the area

Make sure that local libraries, museums and archives are aware of your study. Some may allow you to display a small poster or find room for flyers. Contact with local genealogical societies is key. Perhaps you could offer to write an article for their journal. The local church might be willing to allow a discrete notice on their notice board.

3. Establish a social media presence

Many family and local historians interact on various social media platforms. It is highly recommended that you publicise your one-place study in this way. If you are uncomfortable with social media, maybe you can co-opt an assistant to do this for you.

This step is not just about advertising the existence of your study. You also need to consider how you will preserve and share the results of all your hard work. This will probably take two forms. There will be the transcriptions and databases that you will make, as a result of step four; there are also the more detailed analyses that you will produce as you progress through steps six to eight.

Preserving and Disseminating your Information

It is a good idea to look at the many ways in which other one-place studiers preserve and disseminate their work and see what might suit you. You may well want to use several of the following options.

1. Books

Writing a book can be a daunting prospect but it is a good way of putting together everything that you have discovered about your place. In a sense, that is part of the problem, as such a publication implies that you have gathered all there is to be found. If you discover more material that you want to add, you will have to write volume two. There are other considerations before you decide to produce a glossy publication. This can be costly; it may be many years before you recoup your financial outlay and indeed you may never do so. You also have to decide if you have sufficient space to store a stock of books.

There are ways of overcoming some of these problems. You could opt for an ebook, which is free to produce and distribute. It is also possible to update the information at any stage. Alternatively, there are methods of uploading books to various websites and when orders are received, a copy will be printed on demand.
https://kdp.amazon.com/en_US/l/print-on-demand

www.ingramspark.com/plan-your-book/print/print-on-demand
www.selfpublishingbooks.co.uk/Self-Publishing-a-Book/Print-on-Demand

Alternatively, you could produce a series of booklets on different aspects of the history of your place. Although these do not look so lavish as a book, the cost and storage problems are diminished. It is also more practical to publish something when a small, specific aspect of your research is completed.

2. Articles

Articles are really a smaller version of books and as such are easier to produce. Genealogy and local history society magazine editors may well welcome submissions about aspects of the history of your place, especially if you focus on the people.

3. Websites

Many one-place studiers have a web presence and this is certainly advised. This can be anything from a static page that announces the existence of your study, to something much more complex that may give visitors to your site access to all your data, as well as providing articles and more detailed information. Do look at a variety of one-place websites, to see which aspects you would like to replicate and which you feel you would prefer to reject.

You can create a serviceable website free of charge and without any knowledge of computer coding. Free website builders include Wordpress www.wordpress.com, WIX www.wix.com and Blogger www.blogger.com. If you perform an internet search for 'free website builder', you will find that there are many other options. Try talking to people who use these platforms and looking at the websites that they have created, in order to decide which may suit you.

See also the Name and Place option www.nameandplace.com, which has been developed specifically with one-place studiers in mind.

Some One-Place Websites

Alpha and Jericho, Queensland, Australia www.alphajericho.com.au
Ardchattan, Argyll, Scotland http://ardchattan.org.uk/archive
Bratton Clovelly, Devon, England http://brattonclovellyops.com/wp
Bubwith, East Yorkshire www.bubwith.net

Buckland Brewer, Devon, England https://bucklandbrewerhistorygroup.wordpress.com
Carnamah, Western Australia www.carnamah.com.au
Coldringham, Berwickshire, Scotland https://coldinghamoneplacestudy.org
Gravesend, Brooklyn, New York, United States https://gravesendgazette.com

Springhill, Rossendale, Lancashire, England www.springhillhistory.org.uk
Valcartier, Quebec, Canada https://valcartiergenealogy.com
Wing, Buckinghamshire, England http://wing-ops.org.uk

The focus on British studies in the above list is a reflection of the fact that one-place research is a more established discipline in this region.

4. Blogs

Blogs can be a stand-alone way of disseminating information about your research, or part of a more extensive website. Blogs tend to be short 'essays' or news items, ideally accompanied by a copyright free illustration. Blogs are normally added to on a regular basis; so, if you opt for a blog, make sure you have plenty of material lined up for future posts. All too often, bloggers begin with enthusiasm and regular posts, only for the blog to stagnate when the author runs out of new ideas.

5. Podcasts

Podcasts or YouTube videos have a wide appeal but need a certain amount of expertise to produce. This format is becoming increasingly popular. If you put 'how to create a podcast' into a search engine, you will find a multitude of self-help guides. Many of these are glorified adverts for different platforms but are useful nonetheless.

6. Exhibitions

Staging an exhibition is an excellent way of engaging the present day inhabitants of the community that you are researching. With luck, visitors will come armed with photographs and memories to share, so make sure you have methods of copying or scanning photographs and documents on the spot. Memories are better recorded on a separate occasion but this is a good way of finding potential interviewees. Producing display materials that look professional and copying pictures and documents for exhibition purposes can be expensive, so bear this in mind. It is also more difficult to arrange an exhibition, with all the necessary advance publicity, if you live at a distance from your place.

7. Talks

Giving talks about aspects of the history of your place is another good way of spreading the word and encouraging others to contribute information. You will be expected to produce visual aids, probably in the form of a power-point presentation. Genealogy societies and more general social clubs may well be keen to invite you to address their group, providing you can deliver a slick performance.

Step 10 - Enthusing Others

If you have worked your way through nine steps, or even just two or three, you will have found that one-place studies have become an obsession. Now is the time to enthuse others and spread the word about this exciting brand of research. This is particularly important as the more one-place studies there are, the easier and more meaningful step eight becomes. You may have chosen an ancestral area to study yourself but almost certainly, your ancestors were also connected to many other areas. Hopefully, as one-place studies spread, people will adopt the other places that appear in your own ancestry.

Whilst you are working on step nine, publicising your own study, you can also share information about what one-place studies involve. You can do this in many ways, from a brief social media post, to writing an article for your local genealogical society journal, explaining how one-place research works. You can advertise your own study in the process.

So, as I contribute to my own step ten by writing this booklet, I would like to wish you well with your own one-place journey.

Janet Few 2020

You may be interested in the online course *First Steps to a One-Place Study* run by Pharos Teaching and Tutoring www.pharostutors.com. This covers similar material to this booklet with the exception of step seven, which is beyond the scope of the course. It also provides encouragement, advice and motivation through tutor guidance, the completion of short exercises and interaction with other students. In addition, Pharos run a more specific course *Discovering Your British Family and Local Community in the early 20th Century*, which encompasses one-place techniques. Both of these courses use British sources as examples.